. November 1979. The great Galilee Bell of Durham is about to be painstakingly lowered 180 feet to the ground at the start of an operation to remove ll eight bells so that a new steel bell frame can be installed, replacing a 200-year-old wooden frame made unsafe by rain, snow and woodworm. Experts rom the Whitechapel Bell Foundry in London were called in to ensure that the operation ran smoothly. A powerful winch, hung on steel girders specially tted into the bell tower, lowered the 1·5 tonne tenor bell on a massive chain through a hole in the roof of the nave with only three inches clearance all ound.

2. Tommy Mackin took this picture in 1984 of a miners' rally that replaced the traditional Gala. It is said that Durham looked like a city under siege as town centre pubs stayed closed and shops put up their shutters. Police kept a low profile as around 10,000 people marched through the city in what was the biggest protest march of the pit dispute. It turned out to be a reasonably peaceful affair; there were only three arrests, for disorderly conduct obstruction

# Durham City
# in Focus

3. An *Evening Chronicle* photograph from July 1952 of the Durham XI which gave such an outstanding performance against the Indians at Ashbrooke. *Back row, left to right:* M Tate, J H Clarke, A W Austin, K Williamson, T K Jackson, N W Owen. *Front row:* R Aspinall, H D Bell, R B Proud, J Keeler and A Coxon.

# Clive Hardy

First published in 1991 by
Richard Netherwood Limited
Fulstone Barn
New Mill
Huddersfield
HD7 7DL

in association with

The Newcastle Chronicle & Journal
Thomson House
Groat Market
Newcastle-Upon-Tyne

Printed in Slovenia by
Gorenjski tisk p.o.
Kranj

Designed by Clive Hardy

ISBN: 1 872955 10 X

4. Durham Market Place on a snow-splattered morning in May 1963.

# Introduction

The book, the last in the *Evening Chronicle's* look around the north-east, concentrates on Durham City though there has been a little straying from the straight and narrow to include Sherburn, Shincliffe and the old mine at Finchale. This is not a history book in any accepted sense of the word; it is a book of photographs with what is hopefully a little historical information added on. The book has only one objective – to entertain, there is no message to propound. So magnifying glass out and nostalgia caps on!

This book would not have been possible without the efforts of journalists and photographers past and present including: Tommy Mackin, Malcolm Hepple, Paul Dodds, Geoff Hewitt, Paul Norris, Eric Burns, Stuart Outterside, Lawrie Wilson, P Schaill, George Swift, D McStea, F Hulme, J Napier, Dick Jones, W R Gray, Ian Robson, Ian Woodhouse, John Tunney, David Whetstone, Arthur Steel, D Webb, Mike Blenkinsop, D Denholm, Alan Haydock, Walter Rich, Denzil McNeelance, Eddie Brown, Maureen Cozens, Fiona MacBeth, Oswald Peterson, Alan Southwell, Ian Winter, Fraser Davie and Suzanne Heron. Special thanks are due to Sandra Ramsdale and Dennis Forman and his team at the Newcastle Chronicle & Journal.

5. The Freemen of England parade through the centre of Durham in September 1988 after attending an historic service in Durham Cathedral. More than two hundred freemen, some in colourful ceremonial robes, were led from the cathedral to Durham Town Hall by the Mayor of Durham, Councillor Mrs Mildred Brown, and her bodyguard of pike-bearers. A musical accompaniment was provided by Bearpark Brass Band.

6. Pity Me from the air in January 1982. On the left is Front Street, on the right is the Pity Me bypass, and just sneaking into the top of the picture is Framwellgate Moor. Photograph by Stuart Outterside.

7. The signpost becomes an apt title for this photograph from February 1983.

9. This picture was published in the *Evening Chronicle* in December 1955 as part of a special feature on the increasingly dangerous (for pedestrians and motorists alike) Great North Road and the pressing need for solutions to be found.

8. *Left:* Small boys perspiring in the sunshine deal manfully with a pin-point puncture in one of their cycles. And the original caption for this 1961 picture? "A pitiful place for a puncture!"

10. In March 1977 this dilapidated building at Harbour House Farm, east of Framwellgate Moor, was featured in the *Evening Chronicle* after being identified as a unique medieval chapel. The building, 25ft × 12ft, was the private chapel of the Forcer family for four hundred years up to the 1800s. In the picture is three-year-old John Bell, son of farm manager Mr Kenneth Bell.

11. A self-help scheme for the residents of Newcastle Terrace and North Terrace after the council refused to do anything about the disgraceful state of the road. Dressed for the part in this 1978 picture by Geoff Hewitt is six-year-old Narmi Lamsdaine.

12. January 1978 and the residents of Durham Terrace, Garden Avenue, Tindale Avenue and Newcastle Terrace form the Old Framwellgate Moor Residents' Association in direct response to the Durham District Council's withdrawal of improvement grants. The trouble had started in the summer of 1977 when the council served demolition orders on numbers 4-9 South Terrace, maintaining they were unfit for human habitation. Effectively, the council's withdrawal of improvement grants for the remaining properties meant that the council considered that the houses would not last another 15 years – though they'd already been up nigh on a hundred years.

13. Front Street, Framwellgate Moor, December 1963.

4. The Salutation, an easy-to-find pub in an out-of-the-way location at Framwellgate Moor. Easy to find in 1988 simply because if you couldn't see it, ou'd certainly hear it! The Sally catered specifically for students from the nearby college and the younger element from County Hall and Durham County olice Headquarters.

15. Described by some – probably many – as a monolith of concrete and plate glass, Durham County Hall, June 1969.

16. Celebrating the opening of their Victorian bar at the County Hall in May 1978 are (*left to right*) comedian Dick Irwin, Graham Stephenson (general manager) and Jennie Donohoe (functions manager) with other members of the staff.

17. The Durham Light Infantry Museum, October 1988. The regiment was raised in 1756 as the 68th Foot and in 1808 was one of the units selected for training as light infantry.

Four years later, the 68th gained the battle honour Salamanca which was followed in 1813 with Vittoria, Pyrenees, Nivelle and with Orthes in 1814. The 68th saw service in the Crimea and was in action at Balaclava, Alma, Inkerman and Sevastopol.

Under the army reforms of 1881, the 68th and the 106th were amalgamated to form the 1st and 2nd Battalions, Durham Light Infantry. The 2nd Battalion had had a particularly exotic history by north-east standards. It was originally raised as the 2nd Bombay European Light Infantry, in the private army of the Honourable East India Company, becoming the 106th Light Infantry in 1858 when the British Government took over responsibility for India.

18. Some of the exhibits housed in the DLI Museum including the gun used by Adam Wakenshaw VC. Wakenshaw, a private in the 9th Battalion, was posthumously awarded the VC for his outstanding courage at Mersa Matruh on the 27th June 1942 when the two-pounder gun, of which he was a crew member, became involved in a short-range duel with an enemy light gun. As the duel developed, all the crew of the DLI gun became casualties, but Private Wakenshaw, despite having his left arm blown off, crawled back to the gun and managed to fire five more rounds which slightly damaged the enemy gun and destroyed its tractor unit. However, the enemy managed to get off a shot, which though a near miss, killed Wakenshaw's aimer and blew him from the gun. Yet despite his severe wounds Wakenshaw once more crawled back to the gun and was preparing to fire when he was killed by a direct hit.

19. The medals of Henry Lee bear witness to the variety of postings a battalion could undertake. Lee joined the army at the comparatively late age of 34, but during his twenty-one years with the Colours he saw active service in the Crimea, Burma, New Zealand and India. The extent of the empire presented the army with a major headache as to the best deployment possible given the number of troops available. In 1854 when Lee enlisted, the strength of the army stood at 152,780 officers and men – not all of whom were fully trained. Of these, some 28,955 were stationed in India and paid for by the East India Company, but the conquests of Gwalior, Scinde and the Punjab meant that some battalions faced twenty or more years continuous service on the sub-continent where a soldier was just as likely to die from disease as from battle. In the 1840s the 78th Highlanders had lost three officers, 532 other ranks, 68 women and 134 children to disease in just eight months in Scinde. That Lee survived twenty-one years owes much to his own stamina and a certain amount of luck

HENRY LEE
He was born in Rugby in 1820, but did not enlist in the 68 Light Infantry until June 1854. He went to the Crimea the same year and fought in all the main actions and was slightly wounded on several occasions. He served with the 68 LI in Burma, New Zealand and India, during his 21 years in the Army, rising to rank of Sergeant in New Zealand. He was discharged in 1875 with the Long Service and Good Conduct Medal. In 1905, he was awarded, with a gratuity of £10, the Meritorious Service Medal. Henry Lee died in Barnard Castle in 1913, aged 93 years, and is buried in the Parish Churchyard.
Crimea,New Zealand,LS & GC,MSM,Turkish Crimea.
No.951/1-5. Donor  Mrs F Lee (widow).

20-21. *Above:* Officers and NCOs of
Durham Militia at Barnard Cas
c1860. *Left:* Warrant Officers and NC
at the Militia Barracks, Durham, 18
In 1808 the government created
Local Militia, in which every ab
bodied man was liable to serve for fe
years should his name be drawn ou
the hat. The Local Militia survived u
1816 when it was disbanded. Not to
confused with the Local Militia was
Militia, an organization consolidate
1802 with conditions of service clea
laid down. The Militia was organized
a regimental basis, usually by cou
though small counties or coun
having sparse populations might f
themselves grouped together to fo
one regiment such as the Invern
Banff, Elgin and Nairn Militia. Bein
the Militia could prove fatal, as n
could find themselves transferred to
regular army for service at home
overseas. In 1815 the Militia was dise
bodied and, apart from reactivation
some units during periods of civil un
such as the Reform Bill Riots
remained virtually in abeyance u
1852.

Militiamen took life fairly seriou
they had little choice especially as t
could end up serving with a regu
battalion. They were armed and dres
as regulars, the 1852 Militia
requiring men to undertake twenty-
days training (extendable to fifty-si
year and a minimum of five years
vice. In 1853, fifty-two militia infa
regiments were in existence, compris
38,585 officers and men, and there w
eleven militia artillery regime
comprising 3,500 gunners.

23. Photographed at Kings Cross in May 1958 on their way to Durham to attend the bi-centenary celebrations of the formation of the Durham Light Infantry are Sergeant J E Wood (*standing at back*) and (*left to right*) Sergeant E J Parker, W Ibbotson, and Colour Sergeant Daisy Jones.

22. *Right:* Six of the DLI VC heroes. *Clockwise from top left:* Michael Heavyside, Arthur Lascelles, Frederick Youens, Adam Wakenshaw, Thomas Kenny and Ronald Bradford. In September 1988 the DLI Museum's new medal room enabled more than 2,000 decorations won by members of the regiment and their forerunners to go on display for the first time.

24. Parade of troops, thought to be the 68th Light Infantry, taken in India 1870.

25. "Faithful Durhams" say farewell – the 1st Battalion crosses Elvet Bridge on their way to the cathedral in July 1952 prior to embarkation for Korea.

27. August 1983 and the tenth military vehicle rally is held in the grounds of the DLI Museum.

5. It is exactly 12.35pm on the 12th December 1968 and ieutenant-Colonel J H Jacob hands the DLI's Colours to e Dean of Durham Cathedral, as the regiment's 210-year story draws to a close.

November 1988 and the Durhams are reborn due to Her jesty's gracious permission for the 7th Battalion to be tled the 7th (Durham) Battalion the Light Infantry.

29. In February 1990, former batman Arthur Wood became the 10,000th member of the Durham Light Infantry Association after being recruited by his former officer. Mr Wood, of Middlestone Moor, Spennymoor, was signed-up by Major David Bower, the association's secretary. Mr Wood had been the major's batman when he enlisted in the DLI in 1967, a year before the Durhams were merged with The Light Infantry. The Fifties and Sixties witnessed a number of amalgamations partly as a result of the 1957 White Paper on the structure of infantry brigades and partly as a result of the withdrawal from empire. On 23 April 1968 (St George's Day) the Fusilier Brigade became the Royal Regiment of Fusiliers, composed of the former Brigade's four regular battalions and several Territorial battalions. Of the regular battalions the Royal Northumberland Fusiliers became the 1st Battalion, the Royal Fusiliers (City of London Regiment) became the 2nd Battalion, the Lancashire Fusiliers became the 3rd Battalion and the Royal Warwickshire Fusiliers (formerly the Royal Warwickshire Regiment) became the 4th Battalion. The Light Infantry Brigade became a regiment on 10 July 1968 and the Brigade's four regiments, the Somerset & Cornwall Light Infantry, King's Own Yorkshire Light Infantry, King's Shropshire Light Infantry and the DLI, formed the 1st, 2nd, 3rd and 4th Battalions respectively.

30. A striking exhibition of hand-woven costumes made by descendants of the Mayans went on display at the DLI Museum in August 1983. Seventy brilliantly coloured costumes were on display until the 4 September. The Mayan civilisation thrived between 300 and 900AD but in 1983 the descendants were caught in the middle of a war between government and guerilla forces in trouble-torn Guatemala.

31. The renovation of St Cuthbert's House won a certificate of commendation in the 1984 Royal Institution of Chartered Surveyors Conservation Award Scheme. St Cuthbert's House, originally St Cuthbert's Parish Hall, was built in 1898, though in later years it had been used as a decorator's store before falling into bad repair. The building was taken over by Mr Brian Clouston, who designed the conversion, which featured a spectacular glazed end to exploit the view across Durham City from Framwellgate Peth.

32. Marchers arriving at Durham in April 1933 during a means test demonstration.

33. An *Evening World* photograph of the Durham Miners Association building taken in December 1937.

34. The viaduct which dominates the Atherton Street area of Durham. This picture appeared in *The Journal* in June 1969. Showing at the Essoldo was *Ring of Bright Water* and the *Magnificent Two!*

35. Full speed ahead . . .An Inter-City 125 train thunders across Durham viaduct on the East Coast main line in August 1979. The viaduct was in fact built for the York, Newcastle & Berwick Railway's branch line to Bishop Auckland, connecting with the old main line at Leamside. With the opening of this route on 1 April 1857, passenger services on the short branch between Gilesgate Station and Belmont Junction were withdrawn.

36. Durham Station in August 1964, a Victorian building not without character but suffering from the then typical **BR** *malaise* – shabby and uncared for with direction signs, hotel, taxis and other information almost non-existent.

The ornate canopy of the old bus station featured in a 1975 article in the *Evening Chronicle*. It had been hoped that the 1929 canopy would be preserved at Beamish Museum where it would form part of a reconstructed street. However, transport costs to Beamish were beyond the museum's resources and, as Mr Roderick Mackenzie, consultant architect to the United Bus Company, said, "We have always thought that if it was taken down and painted it would look very attractive. To take it down piece by piece would be an extremely lengthy and tricky business as the bus station must remain open and functioning for passengers." When this photograph was taken, no date for demolition had been set.

8. *Right:* Neville Street, c1969.

9. *Below right:* Crossgate in June 1969.

0. *Below:* St Margaret's Hospital, October 1987. Photograph by Geoff Hewitt.

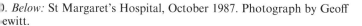

41. In 1961 there was perhaps no public library in the county with a finer view than that from the then new library near Framwellgate Bridge. Built on the side of the river, the view was of the castle and cathedral towering over the steep banks on the opposite side. The lending section of the library opened for business in October 1961 and cost £30,000 to build. Also, 10,000 new books were available for loan.

44. *Opposite page, top:* September 1985 and the influx of new pupils at Durham School, where senior boarding fees then started at £4,800 a year, created extra interest as eighteen girls took their places in the sixth form. Durham newcomers are (*left to right*) Juliet Harris, Joanne Tutungi, Catherine Davis and Lucy Marr.

42. *Below:* Durham School in June 1963.

43. *Left:* Well-kept lawns, stately trees, a dignified old building – a general view of School House and the headmaster's residence in September 1960.

45. *Opposite page, bottom:* Durham School's rugby touring side for the 1987 trip to Canada.

47. Neville's Cross police section office (that's the building sandwiched between the hous[ ]made the *Evening Chronicle* in May 1979 when it was discovered that the premises did[ ]conform to the requirements of the Health and Safety at Work Act. To be strictly corre[ ]not more than three people should have been allowed inside the building at one time[ ]making life difficult for the sergeant and twelve officers based there, let alone when it ca[ ]to interviewing felons or dealing with enquiries from the public. A spokesman for the pol[ ]said "The situation may arise where people have to be asked to wait outside until it is th[ ]turn to be questioned."

46. *Left:* Neville's Cross as it appeared in June 1979. The original cross marking the bat[ ]site (or where the prior displayed the Holy cloth, according to which chronicler you believ[ ]is long gone. It was destroyed in 1589 by "some lewd, contemptuous and wicked person[ ]The remains shown here might well include some original parts.

48. The Duke of Wellington, Neville's Cross, July 1987.

# Battle of Neville's Cross
## 17 October 1346

not to scale

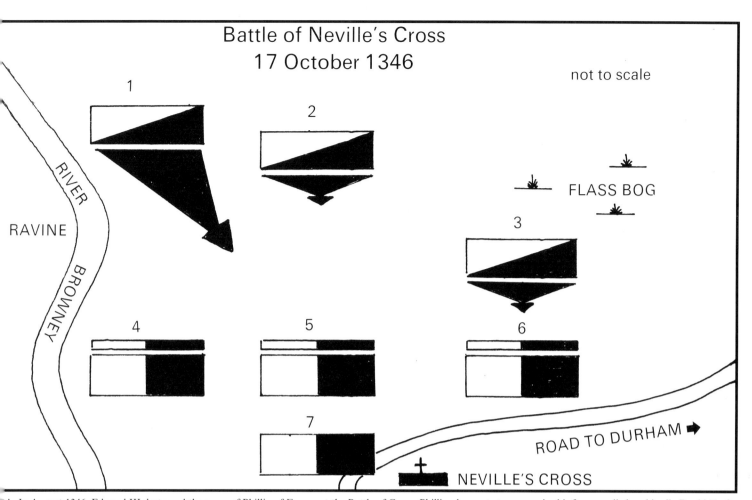

RIVER BROWNEY

RAVINE

FLASS BOG

ROAD TO DURHAM →

NEVILLE'S CROSS

A. In August 1346, Edward III destroyed the army of Phillip of France at the Battle of Crecy. Phillip, desperate to reorganize his forces, called on his ally David II of [Sc]otland to invade England. After a skirmish at Sunderland Bridge, the main forces clashed at Neville's Cross on 17th October. The attack was opened by Archibald Douglas ([1]) who, because of the terrain, was forced to wheel his division to the left, where it virtually merged with King David's troops (2). Both of these divisions suffered badly at [th]e hands of the English archers who were placed out in front. However, Robert the Steward's division (3), charged Lord Neville of Raby (5) and Henry, Lord Percy (6) [fo]rcing them back towards Neville's cross. The tide of the battle was turned when English [ca]valry charged the advancing Scots, forcing them to retreat. It was then that the Archbishop [of] York and Sir Thomas Rokeby's division (4) fell upon Douglas's flank. The arrival of [En]glish reinforcements under Lord Lucy (7) made victory a certainty. King David was [ca]ptured trying to escape over the Browney Bridge.

B. Keeping in the historical vein we have this picture from October 1983 publicising the [op]ening of a unique exhibition tracing the human settlement of Durham from c8,000BC, [thr]ough the Iron Age and Roman occupation to the arrival of the Lindisfarne monks and [the] building of the first cathedral.

C. *Right:* In 1986 King Neptune returned to Durham City following extensive restoration. [Th]e 257-year-old lead statue, commissioned by Geoge Bowes, had lain in a council depot for [a n]umber of years after being damaged by lightning. Restoration work was undertaken by [An]drew and Janet Naylor of Telford, Shropshire.

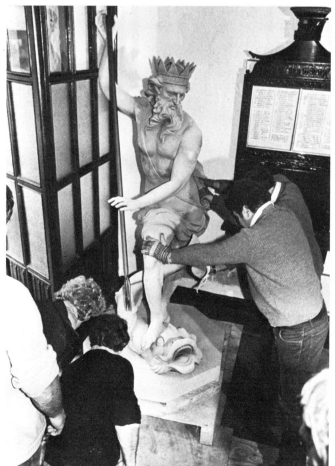

49D. The cathedral and castle from the north in September 1970. It was after the site had become the final resting place for the bones of St Cuthbert in 995AD that the shrine – and eventually the cathedral — grew up. Durham Cathedral: "half church of God, half castle 'gainst the Scot".

50. The old boathouse glistens on a Spring morning in 1938.

. The severe winter of 1895 froze rivers the length and breadth of the country. Here local people skate on the Wear but similar scenes were being enacted on the Trent at Nottingham and the Don at Sheffield.

52. By February 1985 when this picture appeared in both *The Journal* and the *Evening Chronicle*, parts of Durham's ancient city walls were in need of major repairs to prevent collapse. Both Durham County and Durham City Councils arranged studies of the 600-year-old former outer defences of the castle area of the peninsula, not only to determine structural condition, but also to identify the owners of various sections of the wall – a particularly knotty problem spotlighted in 1984 when a section collapsed and needed a £32,000 rebuild.

53. The RAF's only formation display team operating piston-engined aircraft, *The Bulldogs*, fly past the cathedral in July 1976. Based at RAF Leeming, Yorks, the home of No 3 Flying Training School, *The Bulldogs* were about to start their summer season of air displays all over the country. The aircraft were flown by Flight-Lieutenant Dick Fallis RAF and Lieutenant Rod Frederikson RN, who were instructors at the school.

55. *Below right:* Sunshine and shadow in North Bailey, June 1969.

54. *Below:* Not far from the bustle of the main streets the September sun lights the peaceful backwater of the South Bailey with its old church of St Mary le Bow. The half-timbered houses at left are in Dun Cow Lane. The picture was published in *The Journal* in 1960.

56. This striking view taken by an *Evening Chronicle* photographer dates from August 1929. At extreme bottom right of the picture is the perimeter wall of Durham Prison with new houses under construction nearby. But look beyond the railway viaduct where there is little in the way of housing apart from along the Great North Road.

57. An undated *Evening World* picture looking towards the old bailey and Prebends Bridge.

58. The Galilee Bell – recast in 1693 by Christopher Hodson from medieval bell metal – is lowered to the ground during essential work in the cathedral's bell tower in 1979 (see pic 1).

59. By 1979 the old wooden bell frame had seen better days. The two-hundred-year-old construction was in a sorry state having suffered from the combined effects of the elemen and the gourmet appetites of generations of woodworm.

60. *Opposite page, top:* The Rose Window.

61-62. *Opposite page, bottom left:* Looking towards the Rose Window, March 198 *Opposite page, bottom right:* This view by Geoff Hewitt was taken from high up in the cent tower looking down on the centre aisle towards the altar. The photograph was tak through a wide angle lens and shows off the cathedral's magnificent architecture, rank among the finest examples of early Norman architecture in England. The picture w published in *The Journal* in September 1972.

63. Canon Ronald Coppin with t
restored coffin of St Cuthbert
November 1978. Archaeologists spen
year cleaning and remounting t
inscribed oak fragments on a bla
plywood base. The coffin had be
brought to Durham in 995 AD ar
when it was smashed open by Her
VIII's men in 1539, the saint's body w
found to be preserved. The restorati
was carried out by Miss Janey Cronyn
Durham University and Mr Hor
former conservator for the North
England Museums Service.

65. *Opposite page, top left:* In 19
Colours of the DLI housed in
cathedral were taken down
examination and photographing. Al
all 38 flags were involved, the earli
dating back to 1776. In our pictu
Colonel Watson and Lieutena
Colonel John Arnot inspect one of
regimental Colours.

66. *Opposite page, top right:* I's back
October 1986 as a team compris
young farmers, mechanics and cathed
workmen pulled together to get a tv
ton tractor and plough into the Cha
of Nine Altars and up to the font so t
it could form the main exhibit i
harvest thanksgiving display organi
by the Northern group of the Durh
Young Farmers' Club.

64. *Below:* January 1990 and the tomb
the Venerable Bede becomes the fo
point of a major renovation scheme
the Galilee Chapel. Bede, renowned
the father of English history, died in
AD but it was almost 300 years later t
his body was interned at Durha
Bede's tomb has been polished a
special lighting has been installed to p
out the marble slabs and other uni
features such as medieval wall paintir

Pupils of Durham Chorister School in February 1988. Despite the hard work and long hours, there is no shortage of applicants for one of the coveted places in the choir. Rehearsals, practice and services take at least twenty hours a week and the choristers even spend Christmas Day away from home.

68. A corner in Palace Yard, June 1969.

69. September 1964. Morris Men from Bedford perform one of their dances outside the cathedral during a Morris Ring Meeting.

70. Undated photograph taken for the *Evening World* but not published until 1977 when it appeared in the *Sunday Sun*.

71-72. The keep and courtyard of Durham Castle. Both photographs date from 1969.

3. Wing-Commander Albert Cartmell, the University College bursar, inspects the eroded stonework of the gatehouse. The building, which boasts a ne Norman arch, also includes medieval stonework and turreting thought to date from the eighteenth century. In April 1988 it was estimated that storation work would cost in excess of £1·3 million.

74. Students dine in the magnificent Great Hall of Durham Castle, June 1957.

75. The imposing battlements of Durham Castle dominate this picture taken in April 1961. Although the battle of Hastings was decisive and brought the Conqueror to the throne it did not mark the end of the fighting. The northern earls continued to pose a serious threat and in 1069 York was sacked by Danish invaders. Durham Castle was built to keep the north in check and the Scots out.

76. The Durham Festival and Summer School of Twentieth Century Music was only in its second year when this photograph was taken in September 1965. About sixty students attended the school and are pictured here in the Great Hall rehearsing their concert piece, Stravinsky's "Les Noces", which is rarely performed not only because of its difficulty but also because it requires four pianos and a whole armoury of percussion instruments. The festival was organized by Mr John Wilks, a lecturer in music at Durham University.

77. The dining room of the Senate suite.
78. A dayroom in the Senate suite.

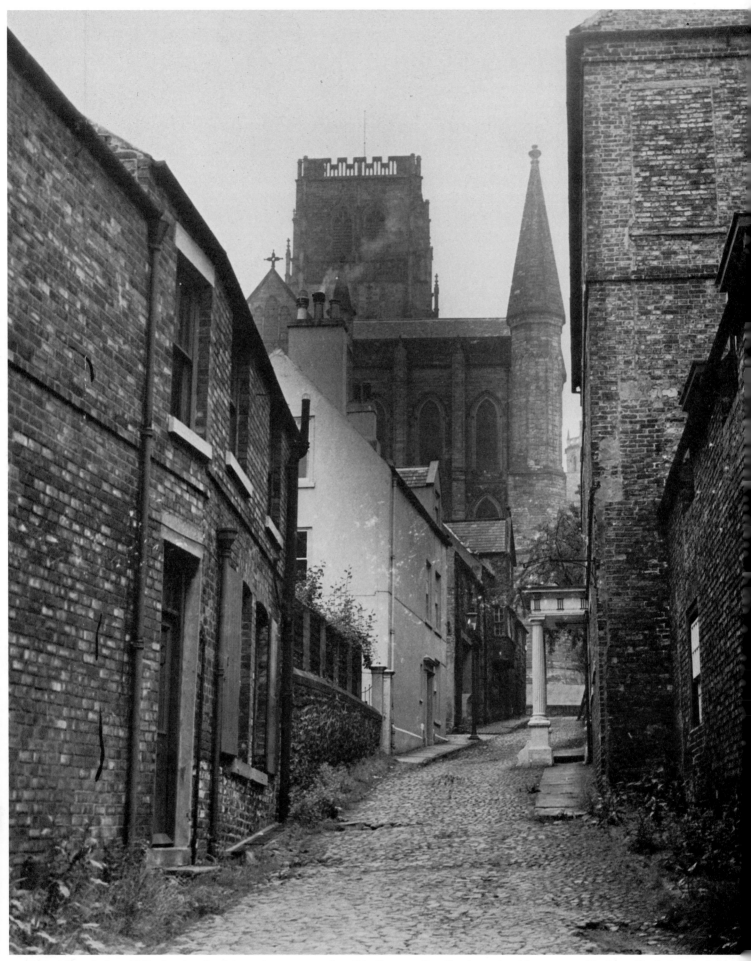

79. Bow Lane in June 1961, showing the eighteenth century portico of the Rectory. Bow Lane was the old entrance to Durham City before the bridges were built.

30. A *Weekly Chronicle* picture dated October 1930 of the old houses on Elvet Bridge. The bridge was completed in 1228 by Bishop Pudsey.

31. *Right:* Cruising down the river on a sunny afternoon? An unusual view of the boathouse taken during the Durham Centenary Regatta in June 1934.

32. The Durham Regatta, June 1975. Here one of the *fours* glides up the Wear beneath the new Elvet Bridge. The £500,000 bridge was given a special mention in the annual awards of the Concrete Society for the way in which it blended in with surrounding concrete structures without clashing with older buildings. The bridge was designed by Durham County's engineer, Mr John Tully.

83. Saddler Street in June 1972. Photograph by Eric Burns.

84. A plaque on a wall in Saddler Street, May 1975.

5. *Above right:* Durham Labour Women's Gala procession makes its way along Silver Street to Wharton Park. July 1949.

6. In 1979 Top Man, the trendy fashion group, took the booby prize, when their snazzy new shop front in Silver Street was voted the environmental ss of the year. Durham City Trust reckoned the outfitters' modern image frontage clashed with the aims of a conservation and tourism area, though fairness they did admit that it was better than the previous occupier, Burtons.

87. This photograph has been published a number of times in the *Evening Chronicle*, and though the zinc block for printing dates from June 1932, the photograph itself might have been taken in January 1930. The young man at bottom right is reporter Charles Close.

88-89. Traffic chaos as buses and cars queue to enter Silver Street from the Market Place in October 1960. *Right:* Pre-dating Dr Who's *Tardis* by several years was the Durham City point duty box, used for a pioneering experiment using television cameras to aid traffic control. However, on one occasion the fire brigade had to be called out to tackle a blaze which damaged electrical equipment; on another occasion the box was damaged when it was hit by a lorry

90. The Market Square in September 1979.

91. The Milburngate Shopping Complex takes shape in this *Evening Chronicle* picture from May 1975.

92. Councillor Alan Crooks (*right*) and Laing Construction regional manager Mike Stoney raise their glasses for the topping out ceremony for the second phase of the Milburngate Shopping Complex. May 1986.

93A. An inside view of the award winning Milburngate Shopping Complex, March 1988.

3B-95. Her Majesty's Silver Jubilee visit to Durham City, July 1977. *Above:* Suzanne and Caroline Scott, dressed in Royal outfits, were hoping to present flowers to the Queen when she arrived at the cathedral. Their ingenuity was rewarded as Her Majesty had a few words with the girls. *Right:* Faces in the crowd. *Below:* Her Majesty goes walkabout.

96. A February 1935 view of one of the old streets of Durham City.

97. In *The Curious Case of the Missing Masonry*, the 'victim' was the twelfth century Magdalene Chapel at Gilesgate. During the early month of 1975 the chapel, who's origins are somewhat obscure, had fallen foul to misguided rockery enthusiasts who were slowly redistributing the old building around gardens throughout the area. Durham police pointed out that not only could gardeners be prosecuted for theft but they could also be liable for criminal damage.

98. Firefighters tackle a blaze at St Godrics in January 1985.

99. The frozen Wear, January 1987.

100. Crowds are thin as the South Moor & Holmside Modernaires Jazz Band marches across Framwellgate Bridge during the 1979 Durham Miners' Gala.

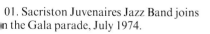01. Sacriston Juvenaires Jazz Band joins
n the Gala parade, July 1974.

102-103. *Above:* Famous faces on the balcony of the County Hotel for the 1987 Gala. However, Labour leader Neil Kinnock and miners' leader Arth Scargill seem to be keeping their distance. Photograph by Tommy Mackin. *Below:* It's back to 1965 for this picture of the then Prime Minister, Haro Wilson, as he moves through the throng congregated on Durham racecourse for the Gala. There were claps and cheers — and a few jeers.

04. This picture of the 1947 Gala contains three of the basic ingredients which date back to 1871 — the banners, bands and the people. The fourth gredient – the beer – seems to be missing but no doubt not for very long.

105. With banners held high, members of Durham women's branches of the Labour Party cross Elvet Bridge on the way to Wharton Park for the Durham County Labour Women's 32nd annual gala, June 1955.

106. Members of the Hylton Lodge in 1971. This picture was published in both the *Evening Chronicle* and the *Sunday Sun*.

107. Old Elvet Station was on the terminus of a short branch line which ran through Sherburn where it joined two other spurs, one to Whitwell Colliery, the other to Blades Wood via Shincliffe. The line then ran via Hetton to Sunderland etc.

108. Shire Hall in Old Elvet later became the university administrative offices.

109. Durham Gaol.

111. *Above:* This picture of Durham Gaol was taken in March 1968 but not published until May 1975 when it appeared in *The Journal*.

110. *Left:* The rules and regulations.

113. *Above:* The prison's catering department was featured on BBC TV's *Food & Drink* programme in 1990. Despite a meagre allowance of less than £7 per prisoner per week, a combination of careful planning, flair and imagination resulted in the prison kitchen turning out a range of meals of a consistently high quality. Our picture, however, pre-dates this regime by more than twenty years.

112. *Left:* The maximum security wing was opened in the mid-1960s. Wire mesh separated the first floor cell-lined gallery from the ground floor recreational area. When opened, the block had ten specially-protected cells among the sixty in the wing and there were workshops, a chapel, visiting room, bathing facilities and a library. Special prisoners wore uniforms with broad yellow stripes down the leg and around the chest.

114. Prison officer T Appleton keeps a careful eye on prisoners sewing mailbags, February 1963.

115. *Right:* June 1982.

116. Prison officer's eye view, June 1982.

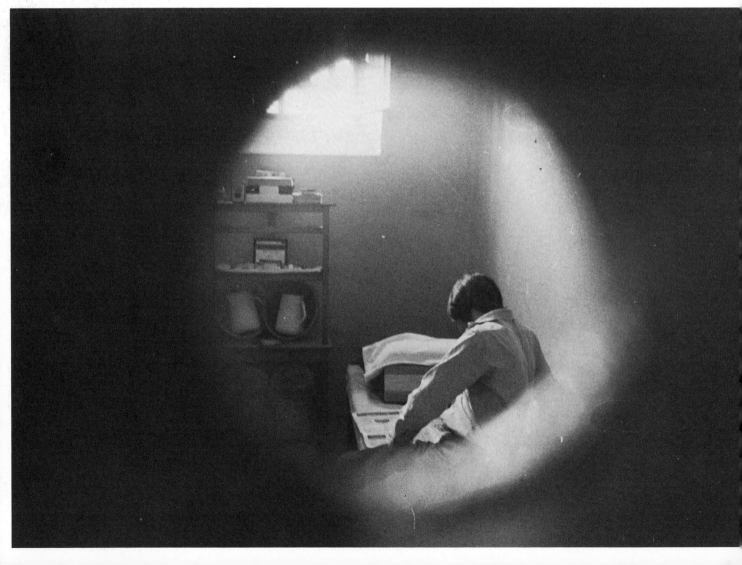

117. *Right:* The exercise area assigned to prisoners in the special security wing, surrounded by a steel wire fence topped with barbed wire. The whole construction was further surrounded by a wall. Now spot the football.

118. *Centre:* Low Newton Remand Centre, intended for young adult offenders aged between 17 and 21, was in the news in October 1971 when social workers voiced concern over the fact that forty-three children were being held in the establishment which is next door to Frankland Prison.

119. *Bottom:* The newly-completed court house in Old Elvet in January 1965.

120-121. Two views of Ushaw College, that great centre of Roman Catholic learning, culture and sanctity atop a wooded hill to the west of Durham. Both photographs were published in *The Journal* in September 1960.

122. *Left:* Hatfield College, photographed in June 1933 when the extension was officially opened by Lord Irwin.

123. St Mary's College in January 1954. The college was officially opened by Queen Elizabeth the Queen Mother on 4 May. *Courtesy:* R L Palmer.

124. Durham's women-only Trevelyan College.

125. Picture by D Denholm of St Hilda's College, taken in May 1960.

126. Christian Petsch (*left*) was one of a group of Europeans who visited the Durham Skill Centre and the School of Electrical and Electronic Engineering at New College in September 1988. Here he is shown robotic equipment by Mr Renwick (*right*) and Mr Edmeades.

127. Meet the smallest police force in Britain – the five men who made up the Durham University police in 1975 were (*left to right*) Tony Isles, Dave Gibson, Ken Harrison, Jack Lake and Barry Millhouse.

128. The splendid chapel in St Chadd's College, October 1961.

129. Durham College observatory was built in 1842 at a cost of £1,400.

130. Elvet Hill Road in the summer of 1959.

132. Sherburn was in October 1960 a typical north country village.

133. The Lambton Arms at Sherburn.

134. Christ Church in the grounds of Sherburn Hospital. The hospital was founded in the twelfth century by Bishop Putsey and was used as a leprosarium. Throughout the Middle Ages, leprosy remained a common and dreaded disease, though to be fair, the name was applied to a number of chronic skin diseases. Lepers were, by the superstitions of the day, regarded as tainted and lived the lives of outcasts. Regulations required a leper to carry a bell to warn others of his, or her, approach.

135. Shincliffe Bridge through the trees on the banks of the Wear. June 1935.

136. Hill Meadows, Shincliffe.

37. The mini maulers of Durham City rugby club's under-nines and under-tens teams beat challengers from all over the North and Scotland to bring back the trophies
1981. The winners are *back row, left to right:* Bob Hockey, Arthur Veide, Doug Pledger, Paul Brady, Alan Readdie and John Oliver. *Third row:* David Lee, David Lund,
yan Stead, Mark Westcott, Mark Valentine, Stephen Readdie, Peter Clark. *Second row:* Andrew Rivers, John Coffell, Peter Middlebrook, Karl Pledger, Jason Ling,
n Richardson, Daren Marrs, Gareth Hockey, Gregory Bradey. *Front row:* Phillip Smith, Michael Nickle, Michael Veide, Daren Ling, David Morgan, David Oliver,
rant Hamilton and Mark Veide.

8. Durham's squad for the 1989 Toshiba County Championship Final against Cornwall at Twickenham. *Back row, left to right:* Mike Boyd, Phil de Glanville, Graham
aisbitt, Mike Fenwick, Steve Kirkup. *Middle row:* Andy Harle, Bryan Dixon, John Howe, Dave Mitchell, Alan Brown, Bill Mordue, Maurice Douthwaite. *Front row:*
raeme Kell, Graeme Spearman, Steve Havery, Ian Dee, Jon Bland (capt), Owen Evans, John Stabler, David Cooke and Phil Joyce.

139. Kent vs Durham, January 1989. Durham hooker Mike Fenwick battles through supported by Andy Harle (headband) and Bryan Dixon.

140. In 1986 a team from St Stephen's School, near Auckland, New Zealand, fielded two teams for matches against Durham School. St Stephen's is renowned throughout New Zealand for its rugby tradition and boasts 14 teams. The rugby line-up in our picture is *left to right:* Stephen Whitfield (Durham, vice-captain), Dallas Seymour, Wiremu Maunsell (captain) and Lee Lidgard from St Stephen's, and Nigel Swales, Durham captain.

141. Rugby action, January 1989. Sheffield University winger Mike Bloo crashes over the line for a try in the UAU Championship clash wit Durham University at the Racecourse Ground.

143. *Opposite page, bottom left:* Peter Stronach played for Sunderland York City, Bishop Auckland and North Shields before joining Durhar City.

142. The Durham City FC line-up for 1971-72. *Back row, left to right:* Arnie Alton, Malcolm Pringle, Chris Thompson, Joe Raine, Keith Adamson, Mick Marley. *Front row:* John Shergold, George Brown, Ray Wilkie, Neal Walton, Dave Rutherford, Tony Cassidy.

144. Durham City FC player-manager Peter Feenan gets his side all geared up for the 1982-83 season thanks to Davro Precision Engineering. Feenan went along to Lou Henry Sports in Gosforth High Street to receive the gear and in the picture are *left to right:* Lou Henry, Dave Thompson of Davro, Feenan, and Dave's partner Lawrence Thompkins.

145. *Overleaf, top left:* Durham striker Geoff Hart during his days at Blyth.

146. Durham City CC players of the Durham Senior League, June 1956. The group include
R Inglis, M Lax, G Draycup, M S Kyle, R Aspinall, S G Sweet, W L Gatenby,
Barnfather, G L Rodham and J Brown.

147. Durham's cricketers celebrate their Minor Counties championship win. With them is ex-England Test star Basil D'Oliveira (*fourth from left*).

148. Archers take aim at the Graham Sports Centre, Maiden Castle, near Durham City. August 1988.

149. Competitors in the 1973 (139th) Durham Regatta. The regatta, the oldest in Britain, had a change of course because of work on the new Elvet Bridge. A total of 182 crews from all over the country took part – an increase of 37 crews on the 1972 event. The regatta originated as a celebration of Wellington's victory at Waterloo.

150. A summer scene from the 151st annual Durham Regatta. A record number of more than 300 entries took to the Wear to contest silver trophies worth a total in excess of £30,000. The regatta's blue riband event, the Grand Challenge Cup, was won by Newark Rowing Club who beat Durham University Boat Club by two lengths.

151. I know this photograph is outside the city limits but nevertheless it captures the spirit of what the county used to be about – mining.
This picture was taken at Finchale, date unknown.